THE BEST DOG
I NEVER
OWNED

THE BEST DOG
I NEVER
OWNED

Amber Hennessy

ISBN 978-1-7374269-0-5 (paperback)

ISBN 978-1-7374269-1-2 (eBook)

A dog cannot relate his autobiography;
however eloquently he may bark, he cannot tell you
that his parents were honest though poor.

– Bertrand Russell, *Human Knowledge.*

TABLE OF CONTENTS

PREFACE

THIS IS THE STORY OF A DIFFICULT DOG. NOT THE WORST, not the meanest, not the one with the saddest backstory. It is not a dog training book. I have no training credentials and as you'll read, most of it recounts my many mistakes and misadventures in figuring out how to best care for a dog that came to me with issues. This is what makes it a fun story (I hope!), but also disqualifies it as any kind of dog advice guide. I do believe that dogs are happiest when they can exercise some autonomy over their choices, but sometimes Baxter had too much freedom. If you're reading a section and you can't believe that I did *that*, please silently roll your eyes, turn the page, and hope that I've learned to do better. I quite possibly have.

Baxter taught me so much in our 12 years together. I started writing this longhand in a blank notebook the day after he died. At that point, I could barely see from tears of heartache, but turned to writing to walk through the loss. I wrote to reflect on our journey together.

Three or four handwritten pages later I realized

there was still so much to tell. I furiously filled that notebook as more stories emerged from my memory into rough sketches of the biggest moments of our shared life. Along these last seven months of filling in the details of those stories, family and friends have offered me so much support, even reminding me about some of the funnier incidents that I had forgotten until they reminisced with me about him. Thanks to everyone for sharing your memories about him with me.

What you'll find here can best be categorized as the true adventure story of a young woman who just had to have a dog, and the frustration, the embarrassments, and the joy that brought me along the way. This book is for everyone whose heart has ever been owned by a dog.

HUGH

HUGH WAS AN 80-POUND POOFBALL OF FLOOF, AND I loved him instantly. True to a husky's independent nature, he wasn't the best-behaved dog during the one weekend I dog-sat for him. His nose found my house-mate's fancy bacon-infused chocolate bar and he stole it off her desk. He shed all over the house. He pulled me along city blocks and trampled over my other house-mate's delicate, careful gardening in our tiny strip of a yard. He slept on my bed. In that short weekend, he filled a void I wasn't even aware I had been missing. It was heaven. I wanted Hugh to come stay with me every time his owners were away.

At that time, I was living with friends found via Craigslist, or more accurately strangers who had become great friends. All three of us were living peacefully in their rowhouse in the Shaw neighborhood of Washington, D.C. in 2007. I was finally living amidst the bustle of city life instead of just passing underneath it all via the Metro every day. Commuting to and from my office as a young 20-something, this route felt energizing and fresh – each day was an adventure. Outside of work, I was making more new friends than ever through my housemates' avant-garde theater company. The only problem now was that all my new friends were human, but I craved a canine connection. Through dog-sitting, I rationalized I could have almost all the benefits and none of the costs of having a dog. Problem solved!

But the following Monday, after Hugh the Husky had gone home, the law was laid down by my housemates. NO DOGS ALLOWED. I don't recall if I had asked their permission before taking Hugh on as my new best dog friend, or if the idea was green-lit up until an 80-pound, shedding, slobbering, non-paying housemate with no regard for personal space or possessions solidified for them the reality that they did not want to live with a visiting dog.

Living under the Dog Ban, my fixation to have a dog only continued to grow. I had been given a small taste of what having a dog could be like, and I longed to make it a more permanent reality. While I had to respect their wishes, I didn't have to live with their decision. But I had no leverage here since I was just renting a bedroom in their house. This was the neon arrow pointing to the Exit sign. It was time for me to be moving out of our shared home.

I engaged a realtor, and she found me a sunny one-bedroom upstairs apartment of my very own about seven blocks away from the current place, in the Bloomingdale neighborhood. I went from spending several hundred dollars a month on rent to over a thousand dollars by signing this lease, and from living in a shared space with housemates to living totally alone for the very first time in my life. Making this move meant my living arrangements became more established and grown-up. A real independent adult? This was at least a significant milestone on the way towards adulthood. I empowered myself to make these major life changes with the full intention of filling any loneliness of the space with a Dog.

I had been dreaming about herding dogs: border collies, kelpies, cattle dogs, shepherds. I was drawn to their energy as potential running partners but understood the foolishness of keeping a high-intensity, working breed type of dog in a one-bedroom DC apartment while I worked at the office full-time. Still, when I went to fill out the rescue application, these are the types of dogs I put on the blank line near "Interested Breeds". Surely the shelter wouldn't send me anything more than I could handle, right?

I knew it would be worthwhile, but I was still nervous. What if I really couldn't handle a dog with my work schedule? I knew it was a big responsibility and planned to budget for a dog walker as well. I was already spending so much more money just for the apartment, so I worried about all the additional costs of caring for a dog – food, toys, supplies, monthly preventative medications, vet care, the dog walker – it all added up to a significant sum. This is why when I submitted my application, I reached the sensible decision NOT to adopt a dog right away, even though I was making this big move to accommodate one. Instead I decided that I would foster first.

Fostering is intended to provide a temporary shelter for pets in a low-stress home environment where they can wait for a permanent adopter. It often provides a lifeline to get more pets out of shelters and can last anywhere from a single overnight to as long as it takes to find the right home for a pet. The shelter can sometimes be too stressful, noisy, scary, or lonely for dogs and this can cause negative behaviors, making a successful adoption that much more difficult. Plus, the entire time you are fostering, the pet remains legal property of the shelter or rescue group. They will cover all veterinary costs, monthly medications, and sometimes even provide food or other supplies for the pet. The fact that I could help an animal find a great home while having a financial safety net to rely on before I was fully confident in my new budget was a double-bonus that made fostering the perfect first step.

Now, we've set the stage. I've signed the lease and have semi-settled into the new apartment. Looking around the two rooms, a bed, a desk, a folding card table, and a World Market futon topped with an overstuffed ivory cushion filled the space. My boyfriend Andrew, who was away in Florida for work at the time, had encouraged me to apply at the shelter already, so my application to foster a dog was waiting and approved.

I did not choose the dog I got. He was assigned to me. The shelter called. They had a dog who needed a foster home - a 9-month-old black cattle dog/lab mix with a speckled white chest and pointy ears, about 35 pounds. He was nervous and not showing his best side at the shelter.

When could I pick him up?

JAILBREAK

I miss my family. I miss the warm sunlight. It's dark here, no windows to the outside. When the nice people here take me outside for Business Time I am scared too, the street is so noisy and I don't trust the strange people I see. I just want to go home. I hope my family comes back for me soon.

I hate it here. Haven't I been through enough already? First my leg, and now this? Where is my family? I thought this was like the vet, and they would be back for me the next day. But the next day turned into the next and now I'm really scared. Some of these dogs smell so tough. New dogs are coming in here every day. I'm tough. I've got to show everyone I'm tough, so I don't get hurt again. People come look at me in my cage but they're not my family.

Get away from me! Ruff Ruff Ruff!!

One of these dogs has been here for months. She told me she's seen many other dogs come and go. They always either leave with a new person, or sometimes they don't get to leave at all. She told me that my family is not coming back for me. It's not my fault, she says.

She looks so intimidating, but she's kind and wise. Her legs and face are covered in scars. Her person was evil, and now she's waiting here for something called "court" because she is called "Evidence". She says it's much better here than where she was before; she doesn't mind waiting. Her person made her fight against other dogs. One day she lost, so the evil human locked her in a small plastic box and abandoned her. She thought she would die, but she was determined to live and chewed her way out of the box. Then some nice people found her and brought her here, and other people helped save her life. Here she is so grateful because they feed us regularly and we are always clean and safe, and she'll never have to fight again.

DAY 12

Today the nice people who are always here and take care of us came to talk to me – They said I am going to meet a nice Lady. She's never even seen me before. She is going to take me to her home and wait with me there until I find a new family. I'll go. Even though I'm scared.

DAY 14

They say the Lady is coming any minute! Oh but first here is dinner kibbles...nom nom nom...

The Georgia Avenue shelter of the now defunct Washington Humane Society was located in a typical DC brick rowhouse, that later expanded to two adjoining rowhouses that were still not connected from the inside. The building had been converted in minimal ways, for example, a secure double-door entrance to the lobby was controlled by a buzzer at the reception desk. But the layout was still essentially that of a regular house, not at all modernized or fit to the needs of a shelter by today's standards. The lobby esthetic was most akin to a high school cafeteria, except there were bunnies or birds displayed in the front window, cats in the lobby, and a dog wash station in the back. A few plastic chairs were squeezed against the wall, set on a pale linoleum floor.

Everything in the space served a dual purpose, especially the staff, and it was very cramped. I was already a regular volunteer here, walking and washing the dogs, so I was familiar with the starkness of the dog kennel housed in the basement. Down a narrow cement staircase with a low ceiling, dim lighting, and no windows, about eight dogs were stored, awaiting whatever came next.

I rang the buzzer and was admitted to the lobby. A shelter worker went to retrieve the foster dog from the basement kennel.

Out of the cage. Up the steps. Faster Faster Faster Hurry Hurry Hurry. No time for good-byes. Yes! We're going to a new door! The one I came in on the first day with my family. Is my family here?? Have they been found? No – The Lady is here! I can smell it.

He was black and shiny, skinny, and slippery like a seal. A tuxedo white-speckled chest, ears pointed straight up in interest and then pinned back in excitement as he bolted towards me across the glassy linoleum, legs skidding in all directions but forwards as he couldn't grab any traction.

Pull Pull Pull! Let me get to her. She will get me out of here. Sniff Snuffle Sniff Snuffle Sniff Snuffle. My body squirming against her in all directions. Circling the legs - around, under, and through. OK, I've done my background check. She's good.

She's safe. Now GET ME OUT OF HERE!!

And we were off.

Living in DC, I didn't own a car and instead made frequent use of a car-sharing membership. These cars are parked around the city at reserved spots. In 2008, membership granted you an RFID card which communicated with a transponder built inside of the vehicle. At your reserved time this would unlock the vehicle, allowing access to the car keys inside. Members were responsible for keeping the cars fueled up and most importantly, clean. The system relied on the members maintaining a high standard of cleanliness, because the driver's seat may not even get cold in between your drop-off and the next person's pick-up of the car. Spills or other messes reported by the next driver resulted in a several hundred-dollar cleaning fine to have the car detailed, not to mention the inconvenience caused for everyone after who planned to use that car.

> Ohhh, I feel sick. Stomach feels wobbly. Lots of turns. I shouldn't have eaten so many kibbles at the shelter. But I didn't know I'd be bumping around in the back of this machine. No, I will not sit down. Too much to see, finally getting out of that place. I never want to go back there. But uuuuggghhh I feel awful.
>
> Phew, we're stopped. Hurry up Lady, I need some

air. Yes, door's opening — bllllarrrcccch. Wow I feel better now. Where to next?

Luckily on this day, no one was waiting impatiently for the car, because as soon as I opened the door, Baxter hopped out and barfed a huge load of puffy, partially digested shelter kibbles all over the asphalt. At least he spared me the cleaning fee.

FOSTER FAILURE

MISSION ACCOMPLISHED. I HAD A DOG (AT LEAST TEMPO-rarily) in my apartment. From Day 1, he knew his name and was perfectly housebroken. As he curled up on my bed that first night, we both had the same feeling. *Home.*

But I knew nothing about keeping a dog, especially a reactive one. He was triggered by everything around us in this busy neighborhood. Everything was unfamiliar and scary, especially kids being kids. Most especially, skateboards. This behavior earned him the unwanted nickname "Cujo" after the Steven King dog character that goes on a murderous rampage, which at the time was not undeserved. He would switch from being a per-fectly sweet, loving dog to a powerful, snarling monster. I couldn't take him for a single peaceful walk where he remained calm the entire time. There was always one skateboard or one unfamiliar sight that sent him off into a dark rage.

I now know that dog trainers refer to this as the Red Zone, a state where the dog's mind totally focuses in on the threat. He can't hear me. He doesn't even know I exist for those seconds. He can't accept treats or commands. My only tool in that exact moment of panic was physical restraint. I pinned his body to more sidewalks than I would be able to recount. I would get down on the ground with him and hold him flat against the sidewalk with one hand on his hind legs and the other on his chest over his front legs, so he couldn't slip out of his collar or harness away from me. In this way I cut off his physical ability to lunge or attack, but his barking and frothing continued in a full panic, eyes straining to stay fully fixed on the passing danger, fighting me with all his strength to get up and neutralize the threat. I did reach out to several dog trainers, but at the time most were charging far more than I had available, and even the ones I was able to get advice from didn't offer much assistance for this specific problem. I knew my solution wasn't the best, but it kept everyone safe in the moment.

It's very important to note that the people he saw during these episodes were simply going about their day. They did not wake up plotting about how to use their cane in a terrifying manner, or which hat would form the most provocative shape, or where to best skate with such a clattering as to send shivers of fear straight into the heart of neighborhood dogs. The neighbors were completely unaware that their presence on the sidewalk would antagonize any dogs. But this is not how it felt to either Baxter or me during his moments of fear. Whenever I saw another person approaching at a distance, I would attempt to assess their threat level from his perspective and take evasive actions. The worst instances were when children were so completely startled that they became fascinated by this crazy behavior and stopped to stare at the rabid dog across the street, which just prolonged the episode. Finally, long after the danger had passed by, the cortisol in his body depleted, and he could begin to breathe again. He could see me again. He was once again sweet Baxter.

> I can't really explain it. It just comes over me like a wave. I don't really remember anything that happens. I know it makes the Lady upset but I can't stop, I don't even know when it's going to happen.

I lived through Cujo-level Baxter so many times in such a short period that I realized this dog had major issues. I grew deeply concerned that any adoptive home would be a failure or worse, could become dangerous. There would not be a happy tale for this dog. As I was typing up his adoption promotion ad for the website, I couldn't figure out an appealing and honest way to write it.

> "Very sweet black lab/cattle dog mix. Weighs about 40 pounds. Enters intense fits of rage multiple times a week."

He didn't seem adoptable to me. If the shelter had the resources to help him at the time, I wasn't aware of them. Today, that exact shelter no longer exists. They've merged with another organization and moved out of the rowhouse. They've modernized both the facilities and their behavior assessment programs. A strong foster support network is in place. There are trainers available to work with these dogs. But this was my first foster dog, and at that time I saw how stretched thin this shelter already was. In my head, and possibly in reality in 2008, I didn't see much help for him there. I thought that if I reported these behaviors to this already under-staffed shelter and said I could not handle him, I would be sending a black dog back to the shelter as the first in a series of unsuccessful placements that I feared would end with him being put down. There are a variety of theories about why pets with all or mostly black fur seem to stay in shelters longer or are harder to adopt out. Regardless of the reasons, these pets are often grouped together by rescue organizations with other 'hard-to-adopt' categories such as pit bull type dogs, older pets, and special needs pets. I couldn't live with the idea that I had failed this animal as soon as I had tried to rescue one. The thought of returning him at this point felt like I was a failure. I should give up on my dream to have a dog. So, I kept quiet and kept working to try to help him.

But this behavior problem was huge and felt uncorrectable. Especially in the middle of DC, where people and kids and tiny wheels surrounded us every-where. Once we walked 15 blocks to an eagerly antic-ipated brand-new dog park, only to find it was directly adjacent to a skate park. I had experience with dogs my entire life growing up, I even showed my childhood huskies for obedience (or more exactly, showed off their lack of obedience) at the County and State Fairs, but I had no experience with fear-based reactivity problems. I was very clearly not the best person to help this dog, but this was the dog I had been handed. I did not want to let him down.

I started exercising with him at calmer times of day. Early mornings were easier to avoid unexpected encoun-ters. Starting from my apartment, we covered swaths of the city on foot in every direction. On early Sunday mornings, DC was unusually quiet. The museums were not open yet, and the suits that jammed the sidewalks from Monday through Friday were at the dry cleaners while their wearers recharged at home, mostly outside of the city center. One Sunday we ran straight down to the center of Chinatown, about two miles downhill, through the low hum of the city just waking up. Buses and pedicabs heaved by on the street like athletes setting their feet up on the blocks, preparing to start the day. Baxter had been living with me as a foster for around three weeks now. As we trotted past the Dunkin Donuts on 7th Street, Baxter caught a scent and wanted to stop. I wanted to keep going; I did. In the next moment, I was holding a leash and a collar, with no dog attached. It took another moment for this to register in my brain as I continued to run. When I looked back, Baxter was standing there on the sidewalk in the middle of Chinatown, uncollared, where his reactivity could spark at anything, but calm for the moment.

Standing about 10 feet away from me, the list of bad outcomes was scrolling through my head like a tickertape. He might decide to bolt, run into traffic, get hit by a bus, or get lost. Worse, his triggers might flip. He might see a skateboard, chase it, then what? Heart pounding in a panic, I stopped, turned, and crouched down. Bunching up all my nerves in my stomach, I hoped to keep them out of my voice. I called his name.

Weird. A second ago, the Lady and I were attached, and then I spun my head around and down and now I'm free. The smells in that garbage can are so yummy. These buses are loud. There's a big group of tourists in matching tee-shirts heading towards us. The Lady looks stressed. Now she's calling to me. Of course, here I am, at your service.

He ran straight to me. I was overjoyed. He was safe. I collapsed to the ground to hug my dog in relief. My dog. He chose to come to me. He chose me. He was my dog. It was time to make it official.

ADOPTED. With just a $30 fee, a signed contract,

and a DC pet license, he was now legally my dog. Plus, such a bargain! People pay thousands of dollars for dogs, but I got this one practically for free!

SCAR

THE VET WAS CONCERNED ABOUT HIS LIMP. ALONG WITH the adoption paperwork for a new dog, I received a certificate for a free initial vet consultation. Perfect! To make use of it, we walked the 14 blocks from 2nd Street to the vet's office on 16th Street. As the vet examined his legs, he asked me questions I did not have the answers for about Baxter's scars. One long scar ran along the middle inner side of his right leg, across the knee joint, and spanned across both the upper and lower leg. At the termination of the scar, his right foot was short of two toes, just like these had been lopped off. The shelter had no records about this, even though he was only nine months old at the time I brought him home. I was too young and inexperienced to question the fact that he must have had a serious surgery not very long ago in his young puppyhood and needed immediate follow-up care that I had been completely oblivious about. That the shelter did not investigate this further before sending him to me helps confirm my intuition that they were not currently operating at peak performance.

This lack of information regarding the Frankenstein scar prompted the vet to order x-rays and a specialist consultation. This was also my first encounter with the terror of the bill due at the vet's reception desk. While the exam was free, the accompanying x-ray, pain medication, and specialist's fee were not. This vet showed me some sympathy and mailed the CD of the x-ray to the specialist, rather than sending us there for an additional appointment. Still, that first total balance due was over $1,000 and this was now fully on my credit card since signing the adoption paperwork. From these investigations we learned Baxter had developed a serious bone infection that would kill him if left untreated any longer.

In shock, I checked out a shared car and drove the 14 blocks home, then spent the next few hours praying for my new puppy not to die. Of course, I called the shelter again to ask about this mystery but found no additional information. The clues the vet and I had gathered:

- 🐾 Baxter had surgery just prior to being handed over to the shelter.

- 🐾 The surgeon inserted two metal rods into his leg to hold the bones together.

- 🐾 He had two missing toes on the leg with the large scar and one missing dewclaw and minor scarring on the opposite leg.

- 🐾 He came to me perfectly housebroken but extremely reactive.

- 🐾 All of this had occurred before he was 9 months old.

- 🐾 None of this information was shared with the shelter when he was surrendered, or else it was not recorded.

Essentially, his body's bone cells were under attack because he was not receiving the post-surgery antibiotics to help his body accept the implanted metal rods. I imagine that Baxter had lived with a very caring family in his early puppyhood. He never should have ended up in the shelter. The family loved him and trained him very well. One day there was an accident with a skateboarding kid. Baxter's small puppy leg was badly destroyed. The injury was severe and expensive to fix. After completing the surgery, either the family decided they could not afford to keep him or realized that he was not a good fit for their active family. I don't blame this imagined family for what happened but I do wish they had shared his medical history at the time of surrender so he could have received the correct follow-up care. Missing those critical antibiotics almost undid the good intentions of the corrective surgery and was nearly fatal.

I don't wish to talk about my former life.

THE SEARCH FOR INNER PEACE

Meanwhile, Baxter was unaware of his health scare. He was fully alert and ready for action at every second. While I was away at the office working full time, plus my commute, which added up to long days away, Baxter had settled into the lonely monotony and was taking his anxiety out on my belongings. I knew nothing about how to keep a dog in this context. I had no crate. I was smart enough to hire a dog walker, but that short 20-minute visit only offered a brief relief from a very boring day for a young, working-breed type dog. He needed something to do, so he made his own work.

Whenever I left for the office, I shut him in the front room after a lengthy morning exercise that ALWAYS included at least one vicious barking encounter (his choice). The room had large windows overlooking the street, so as I walked down the stairs and along the sidewalk towards the Metro I would look up to the window and see his sweet face appear, paws on the sill, ears perked, watching me go.

Sigh. One of THOSE days again. She leaves me so many days and she is gone forever. First job — paws up on the sill. Look cute. Yearn for her to turn around. Catch her eye. Maybe it will work this time? Nope. She just keeps walking further away. Further still, now I can't see her at all.

That's it. The start of yet another dull day. Better than the shelter if we're comparing, but really, I'm desperate for more. At the shelter I had been too afraid to even think about being bored. Now I know about all of the fun things we could be doing but can't do because she leaves me every "weekday" for "work" (her words).

Now, down to serious business. What do I want to destroy today? Let me think. Books — did it. DVDs and CDs — done. Pieces of clothing — maybe tomorrow. Office supplies and important papers? Hmmm hold that thought for later. Ooooh, I know. This will be my greatest accomplishment to date. My masterpiece! Let the shredding begin!! Let the filling fly, this couch will not live to see another day!!! Then she'll get the message straight. Just don't leave me.

I started to cringe before opening the door every day, dreading the clean-up of that day's sacrificial items.

Christmas, 2008. In 2008 I was still printing out directions from Mapquest to navigate to new places.

No Google Maps from my phone, at least not from my cheap phone that was still more phone than pocket computer. Portable satellite GPS systems brought live mapping technology into our hands and our cars, and I was so happy to receive one from my family as a Christmas gift. These units were expensive and were frequently targeted in car break-ins. More carelessly than leaving the unit in my rental car though, I left the box containing this gift in the room with Baxter on my desk, then went out for a date with Andrew that night. The machine had been used exactly one time, to navigate me back to DC from New York. After the date we came back to the apartment to find pieces of a ripped-up box and a chewed-up piece of junk. The screen was cracked and speckly. It would not turn on. Useless. Clearly in his mind, this was the newest toy brought home to please the ill-behaved, now nearly adult dog. This cracking cracked me, and I cried in frustration and sadness. Not just over the loss of my brand-new Christmas present, but because of my increasingly anxiety-riddled dog.

Nothing explicitly changed that night, but it was a turning point in my mentality and understanding of what this challenging dog required of me, and of the structure I was so far failing to provide him. I needed to get serious about his training for the both of us. (And I replaced the GPS out of my own money, never telling my family about this incident until just now.)

One bright idea I had was to start taking him more

places with me. This way he could be less alone when I was out doing activities during my limited free time. We were already walking and running all over the city, so this seemed simple. One evening a week I volunteered at the front desk of a yoga studio. This position didn't pay but the few hours of tending the studio earned me free classes whenever I wasn't working, a great trade-off instead of paying $20 a class. The studio owners were dog lovers and approved for Baxter to join me at my front desk duties. The job was simple – welcome the clients, get everyone registered, and prepare tea for the group to share at the end of the class.

That evening, the welcoming part went smoothly. What a cute dog! So sweet! He received lots of positive attention and praise. The class participants went into the studio behind the Japanese-style sliding doors. The sun went down; the room was softly lit by two rows of yellow wall sconces and candlelight. I had zoned out on Internet browsing and was not paying close attention to the demon at my feet.

After an hour of stretching and twisting, the clients were fully relaxed into a peaceful state of mind and body. But during that same hour while we were seated at the front desk, Baxter's anxiety or boredom had taken over and he had chewed through the nylon of his leash, severing it entirely from the desk leg he was tethered to.

At the front of the room, the Japanese doors slid open to release the class, and through the hazy, dim light, Baxter launched forward towards the threat in full attack mode, startled by the unexpected movement. Barking at the intruding yogis with no restraint holding him back, the now useless nylon leash laid limp on the floor behind him. Terrified shrieks yelped out as the class instinctively leapt back in fear, the group bunching together for protection. The studio's owner rushed forward in horror upon hearing the wild commotion mere seconds after her class session ended. Once he realized these were the same friendly women who had greeted him on the way in, he turned peaceful and calm again. Mortified that my sweet dog had ruined this evening for the paying clients, I did not have to guess about the studio owner's thoughts. Every heart in the room was pounding, but no longer from the workout. No one lingered for tea. The owner and I closed up as usual then she drove me home that night with Baxter, but the silence was thunderous. The words did not need to be said – NO DOGS ALLOWED.

TAKE ME TO CHURCH

DURING THE EARLY 2000'S GENTRIFICATION WAS SPREAD-ing across DC like a winding river, snaking up one street partway before turning and skipping over the next few blocks. My apartment stood on one such demarcating line. Around my neighborhood, carriage houses in back alleyways were being converted into luxury studio apartments and brand-new condos were built inside old brick buildings, while formerly stately mansions were abandoned in property tax arrears to crumble. Go-Go music pumped out proudly from the Metro PCS corner store, lifting the city's spirit for blocks. Bodegas opened to sell fresh fruits and vegetables to fill in some of the food desert, since the closest grocery store was several miles away. A new specialty coffee shop was quickly becoming the prime neighborhood meet-up spot among the young career-minded cohort.

Walking east from my front steps, rowhouses and condos were starting to sell for exorbitant prices, fully remodeled with the latest finishes and features. Walking west from my apartment and occupying most of the same block was a long stretch of city-owned housing, where old window unit air conditioners were unable to keep pace against the heavy DC summers. Directly in between these two clashing extremes, I had rented the top floor of a simple two-story 1940s brick free-standing house with a fenced yard for a reasonable price. Across the street was a condemned school. I'd watch with mild concern when unsupervised children from up the street scrambled over the high fence to enjoy the abandoned play equipment.

Next door to the house was a black Pentecostal church, the True Grace Church of Jesus Christ. Throughout the week, especially on Sunday mornings, the church would come alive with organ music and the Holy Spirit. I loved singing along through my open kitchen windows to the gospel music. The buildings were so close together and the speakers so powerful that I could even take in the sermon from my small back patio. The ladies and gentlemen attending the church always wore their Sunday Best, pastel hats with matching skirt-suits for the women and the men in perfectly tailored suits with bright pops of colorful ties and pocket squares. On a sunny summer Sunday morning I'd most often be seen in my stinky jogging gear. One such morning, after church had played the recessional and the crowd was starting to filter outside for sidewalk fellowship before heading home, a surprised cry went up from the gathered parishioners.

I looked down from my second-story window, at first in interest, and then in horror, as Baxter ran circles around and through the crowd, then up the steps - straight into the church! He must have escaped the yard through a hole in the fence and was immediately drawn to all the activity on the street. Shame-faced, I leapt up and ran outside as quickly as I could fly – thoughts swirling around the larger context of gentrification in a historically black neighborhood, and the darker side of the use of dogs as tools of intimidation and control. As soon as I was out on the street, Baxter popped out from the church and ran another tight circle around the startled crowd and then back towards my call. Here though, he wasn't aggressive or lunging, or even rattled. No, the herding dog in his genes was driving this urge. He playfully circled the flock again, letting loose a few happy barks, full of joy for his newly discovered calling.

Accurately assessing my predicament, a woman in the group took pity on my bright red face, which was glaring and yelling at my uncontrolled dog. In good humor she yelled out over the crowd at full volume,

"HE CAME TO GET SAVED!!"

The congregation around her laughed, and with only one tail tucked, the other one waving quite proudly, Baxter and I hustled back inside.

FOSTER FRIENDS

SADLY, A JOB AT A SHEEP FARM WAS JUST NOT AN OPTION. On to my next brilliant idea for calming Baxter's anxiety – get another dog! Not to adopt, but to pick up fostering again where I had left it back in July of the prior year.

My first true foster dog was a fluffy black chow-chow named Polly. She was a real cuddler. Not quite as housebroken as Baxter, but she did OK. They played together and snuggled on the couch together, and I still did not know about using a crate! Walking these two down the street together was a daily adventure; combined they weighed nearly as much as me. One day I came home from work to find the fur of these two black dogs, especially their snouts and paws, caked in white paint. It was splattered and speckled throughout Polly's long fur and on Baxter's nails and embedded in both of their paw pads. In a panic I searched to trace down the source of the paint. Had my landlord done some unannounced maintenance while I was out? No, the walls were all dry. Then I found the evidence. They had busted into my desk supplies and playfully bit open a bottle of White-Out, having a great time sharing it!

I placed a call to Poison Control (for humans – not knowing where else to call immediately). The kind responder on the line was not authorized to give me official advice about a pet, but she suggested that they were probably OK since the amount ingested would have been minimal. I then spent the rest of the night in the bathtub with these two clowns, picking and combing the individual hair follicles with my nails to scrape off the crusted-on layers of blotting substance. They were both mischievously pleased with the extra attention.

Finally, I gained a little bit of knowledge. My next foster was another fluffy black puppy named Lucky, whose name later changed to Danny Boy, because no dog named Lucky ends up that way according to shelter superstition. This poor boy came to me with a broken leg at four months old and was in a cast. He had to be restrained during the day, so this was how I begrudgingly accepted and learned how to effectively use a crate. Baxter remained free to roam the room, still shredding things on his own, but with the foster friend locked up and offering some company, the destruction began to diminish. Danny Boy's leg fully healed. He ultimately lured in his adoptive people with his unique name and went on to live a marvelous life filled with hikes in the woods of historic New England and so much love. He ended up very lucky after all.

I wish I knew the fates of all my foster dogs. Over the years, Baxter hosted a lengthy chain of visitors. One is still in my life, while the rest I have had to trust in the adoption process and fate. With every dog fostered I gained some new insight into the world and behaviors of dogs. Pollyanna, Danny Boy (Lucky), Paloma, Buster, Charlie, Meggie, Crispin, Leo, Honeybear, Boo Radley (Lilac), and Sonya, you were, or still are, all very good dogs.

Andrew wanted to adopt every single dog I fostered so they would not have to leave, because it was too heart-wrenching to say goodbye. Baxter always knew he was the host of these dogs, welcomed them to his pack, and as a fellow former shelter dog, never once was envious or territorial of their joining us. There were never any issues between the dogs. He and Meggie, a little fox lookalike, just a slight bit smaller than him, had the most fun and mischief. They would bounce around the woods together like pinballs.

Boo Radley, a beagle likely mixed with chihuahua, became pregnant with a litter when she was still nearly a puppy herself and was taken into rescue while her puppies were born and adopted out. After the puppies were gone I fostered her and facilitated her cross-country move to California, where she started her new adopted life with my friend and her other beagle. To this day, she continues to crisscross the United States with her pack.

Quite an accomplished life for a dog that was borderline feral and terrified of people when we first met. While Boo Radley has her own epic tale, this is Baxter's, so we return there. But one last odd fact: Boo Radley and Baxter never met. I picked her up for fostering while Baxter was away on summer holiday in New York.

FRESH AIR DOG

BAXTER LIVED HIS BEST LIFE WITH GRAMMIE AND Grandpa (my parents) in rural Upstate New York. This started out as a way for me to save some money on dog-walkers, to get Baxter out of the hot city summers, and to give my parents the missed fun of having a dog again. Skateboards were at their peak usage during the summer months, and for me it felt like the sanest thing to do was to send him away.

At first, Baxter introduced himself to my parents over the phone. Every time I would call them, without fail, Baxter would find a squeaker toy and start making non-stop squeak-squeak-squeaks the entire time we were talking. He made sure he was part of the conversation! Any other time when I wasn't talking on the phone, he showed no such devoted interest in those toys.

So, my parents knew at least they were getting a handful, and somewhat hesitantly accepted the idea for the visit. Baxter thus began a tradition of spending about eight weeks with them for a summer visit between the

Boilermaker Road Race (the second Sunday in July – the biggest event of the year and a reunion holiday for many Upstate NY families) and the Labor Day weekend. I always drove home to New York for both celebrations. Summers for Baxter quickly meant freedom. Grammie and Grandpa soon shed all hesitancy about hosting him, in fact they looked forward to his next summer's visit. He could go in and out as he pleased without a leash and be doted on all day. We knew he would not run away, though some nights we worried about coyote or coy dog packs and would keep him close by when we heard howling in the back fields.

Oh boy. The country. So many smells. So many critters. What is Grammie making in the kitchen? Bacon?? Wow. My Lady never makes this. This is incredible. Yum yum yum. Now we're going to see the cows. They look like giant dummies. I could boss them around easy. What is Grammie picking off of that plant? These are little round balls. Hmmmm tastes like blue…blue…blueberry? I can pick these myself off the bush. I'm helping.

Ha! Grandpa is kicking that flat ball around. I'll attack that thing. It's nearly half my size but if I run over it with my front legs and then bite down with it under my chest I can get ahold of it. Then I pick it up and shake it to show what a great hunter I am.

Time for a nap in the summer sun, I like to make my fur hot to touch. I love it here.

As my dad said many times, "He was the best dog I never owned."

THE MYSTERY OF THE
DISAPPEARING DOG

WHILE IN NY, BAXTER DISCOVERED SOME GROUNDHOGS living underneath the deck, and he would tunnel under the low wooden boards to stalk them. Around most of the deck there was less than a few inches of clearance between the underside of the deck and grass, with only one spot wide enough where he fit to crawl in or out. Sometimes, after he had been under there for a while, he would start to whine or cry, maybe having forgotten how he had arrived in the tight space. He got stuck under there many times, and I would sometimes need to lay flat on the ground with a flashlight, even a few times in the snow, calling for him to crawl towards me to draw him out. Luckily, we never had to cut through the boards of the deck to extricate him.

Back in Maryland, Andrew and I were still straddling life split across our separate houses. We still had a lot to figure out between us before things could move in one direction or the other. I had moved out of the center of DC, in part because of Baxter's reactivity, and into a tiny studio house in Takoma Park. It was just 444 square feet, but it had a small fenced-in yard for Baxter and the foster dogs. Andrew lived in Greenbelt, about a 25-minute drive away with normal traffic. My routine at the start of our weekend followed a quick pace. After commuting home, I'd zap something for dinner in the microwave, pack my bag, pile everything into the car, including Baxter, and drive the hopefully twenty-five minutes to Greenbelt, though it was usually more due to traffic vagaries. The reason for my rush was that if I arrived early enough, I could catch the end of the open mic night where Andrew performed, while I had a pint and said hello to friends. It was often a crawl along the beltway rather than a drive, so I was usually running too late, but I preferred the nights when I made it to the New Deal Café.

On this warm summer night forces were in my favor and I was happy to arrive in Greenbelt early enough to ditch the car and bike ride down the hill to the café. We kept our bikes locked up in the shed in the backyard. I unpacked my things while I allowed Baxter a few minutes in the yard before I zipped off again. I rolled my bicycle out, locked the shed up, clicked my helmet on, and called out to collect Baxter into the house so I could peddle away.

Crickets. Not a sight or sound from him. Puzzled at first, I looked under and behind every shrub in this little patch of fenced-in grass around Andrew's house. It was after dark, but this was highly unusual behavior from Baxter. He was normally never more than a few feet from me. If he had chased an animal, he would have made a low growl or a lot of barks. My heart rate sped up. The silence and his absence felt eerie, like he had just been abducted by aliens or had been swallowed into a sinkhole down to the depths of the Earth. I started circling around the yard, then around the court, and then out onto the street, calling out his name into the dark. With my every call and his non-response, my worry grew more intensely. The list of bad outcomes paraded through my thoughts - my black dog would not be seen at night and could be hit by a car, he might be off chasing a fox and get lost in the woods, or a thousand other unlikely but no less terrifying possibilities churned out from my brain. A friend was walking by right at that moment, so in my distress I enlisted him in helping me search. Andrew would not be back home for another hour at least and wouldn't have heard his phone over the noise of the café anyway. My determination grew now just as intensely as my worry. I had to find my dog. I was calling out his name over and over, jingling my keys for his attention, walking further and further away from the house and down the street into the dark. I felt lost. I was so confused. It didn't make any sense. Where did he go? How did he go?

I returned to the yard and released my friend from

his conscripted participation in my search. It seemed sure that Baxter must return once he concluded his secret mission. Like a hiker lost in the woods, I decided the best course of action was to stay put and wait.

I stood there quietly in the yard, listening for any sign. Then a faint jingle! His collar tags! Oh, what relief! Now I was onto him. He must have tunneled under the shed while I was getting my things together, and he'd gotten stuck under there. Finally, one piece of this puzzle made sense. I raced into the house and grabbed a flashlight to get a better view of what I would need to dig out in order to reach him. I laid down on my stomach in the dirt to peer under the outbuilding … but no green eyes flashed back at me. It was empty, he wasn't under there. Silence. I wept in frustration. This night pre-dates *Stranger Things*, but today I would say he had passed over to the Upside Down.

Had I imagined the jingling noise? I looked again, more methodically this time, ensuring I examined every square foot of dirt, completely convinced that he had to be under there. Empty. Defeated and thrown back into confusion, I stood up and listened harder.

Then I heard it. The tiniest scratch of claws on wood. I knew in that instant. It finally made perfect sense. My face flushed red again from embarrassment, but I was too relieved to care and no one else was around to see me at that point anyway. I raced back inside the house, grabbed the shed key, ran to the backyard again and unlocked the shed doors. Here at last and all along, was my dear dog, wagging his tail inside the pitch black darkness of the shed. Never questioning my (clearly) intentional decision to lock him in there. Why he never barked just once to let me know where he was in response to my frantic calls, I cannot guess. Why my brain immediately jumped to the wildest conclusions, I cannot explain. That night I just rolled my bike right back into the shed, unclicked the strap of my helmet off my head, and closed the doors once more; keeping a careful eye that the bicycle was the only friend locked outside in the shed that night.

OLIVER

ADDING TO THE LIST OF BEINGS BAXTER DID NOT TRUST:
cats. Cats on the street, cats outside of our house, cats
inside other people's houses – all were part of the enemy
cat army. Relentless barking was the only weapon available, to be deployed either until he was being dragged
away or the enemy cat retreated to a distance out of sight.
Even hidden out of sight was not always a guarantee that
the cat danger had abated.

Even knowing all of this, Andrew and I still chose
to selectively ignore these facts on a warm July evening when we accepted an invitation to a cook-out and
decided that yes, we would bring the dog along.

Oliver the Cat also had a black tuxedo with smooth,
shiny fur (very similar to Baxter's coat, if you can pic-
ture it). He was a large cat and lived an independent
indoor/outdoor life. He would follow our friend across
the neighborhood on foot while he visited us, waiting patiently outside Andrew's house in the bushes for
hours, then would trail along behind him again for the

return trip. A passenger using his human as a passport through rival cat territories. He was by all accounts a formidable and very intelligent cat, who did not deserve the disrespect he received that day at the cook-out.

Before continuing this story, I would like to add that I had considerable hesitation over bringing Baxter to the party. My fears centered on his possible reactivity towards rambunctious children or men wearing strange hats, or whatever Baxter decided was scary that day. But it was easier to bring him than to leave him alone for that long amount of time, and we believed that between the two of us we could keep a good eye on him, so we popped him into the backseat of the Corolla and headed out. The introductions all went smoothly, even meeting the few children who were behaving quietly and not playing wildly at all. My protective guard relaxed a bit, and Andrew and I decided that it would be OK to unhook his leash to let him explore the party.

This is great. Hot dogs, burgers, and buns left around everywhere on discarded plates or dropped by little hands. It's not stealing if you just happen to find it on the ground, or if you're charming enough to get it handed over freely. Why yes, I would like to try this piece of...

Wait. Stop this foolishness. I know this scent well. My olfactory receptors detect a member of the evil cat army. Here! At this wonderful party. How can all these kind humans be so blithely unaware of its presence? It is the hypnotic scent that exudes from every cat, disarming the humans and concealing the cats' agenda for total world domination. Now that I've detected it, I recognize it all too well. I've traced this before, but never so thick and close behind it. I can tell that this scent belongs to Oliver the Cat, a high-ranking general in the cat army. I am truly behind enemy lines here. My duty is clear. I must root out the scourge and protect this pack of innocent, idiot humans before they can be lulled under his spell. I only hope it is not too late.

Focus. He is inside the house. I must find a way to get inside. Let's see. We're in the backyard now, and there's a door right here leading to the lowest level of the house. I'll just wait for a second... Yes thank you human! I DID need to get inside very badly.

Now I'm in the enemy lair. I'll need to rely on all my ninja skills. I feel I've been training for this very moment my entire life. A quick sweep reveals no cat found on the basement level. Up I go. Main level, I'm above the party goers now. They are still safe from the cat here. It must be at the top level. This is it. Deep breath. Up I go again. Here, in the bedroom behind this mostly closed door, he is lurking. The scent is overpowering my nostrils. I can barely remain conscious, but I fight through and push on, under the bed I take one more full snort.

Startled, he's OFF! Narrowly escaping my bite, he is flying down the stairs. I'm hot on his tail, back down the way I had climbed moments ago. Back to the main level of the house. Wait. What's this? He's taking a divergent tactic and pushes through the swinging door that leads out to a covered porch overhanging the yard.

Bang! He's through the door! Bang! I'm through the door! Right after him, he's got to be cornered now on this tiny porch. At the repeated clatter of the swinging door, the party goers look up at us to witness my certain triumph over evil. Yes humans, today you are safe. You are welcome.

Oh no! He is startlingly quick, and there's an escape route I had not foreseen. Oliver the Cat ducks under the railing and leaps the eight feet off the side of the porch and down into the yard full of revelers. I don't hesitate. I don't hold back. I take the same giant leap in pursuit, body flying out into space. Lacking the cat's natural "grace" (some call it, I call it trickery), my legs aren't prepared to catch me from such a great height, humans would say about eight feet. My legs bow out from under me. Thud. My chest thumps against ground in my fall. The wind knocks out of me for a breath, but in the next I pop up, legs set surely under me again. I continue the chase undeterred, but he has now slunk off, disappearing into the dark streets. At least I can sleep soundly knowing that I did everything in my power to protect the humans from the lurking menace this day.

To my great relief and amazement, no bones were broken. The Great Chase left no permanent damage to either pet, but surely lived on in Baxter's memory as the cat that got away, and in Oliver's memory as the mangy dog intruder. He was never invited back. Yet another destination removed from our list: NO DOGS ALLOWED.

INTO THE WOODS

TOGETHER, BAXTER AND I RAN. AFTER A FEW LEVELS OF obedience classes, we both decided it was a bit boring, and moved on to learn the basics of agility. The classes were dynamic and fun, involving running, jumping, and teamwork. He did passably well in the classes for the little amount we practiced. But I wasn't passionate about competing or earning legs in the ring, so I transplanted those skills from the practice equipment out onto the trails. Some combination of agility training and intuition guided him on how to hold the path while speeding around corners, scrambling through obstacles, and jumping over dead trees.

Starting a little distance away from the car on a barely used forest trail, usually on a Friday morning, I would unclip the leash. Baxter would shoot off like an athlete after the starting gun, sticking true to the path, the well-worn scents holding him on the track as he followed the twists and turns of the ways man has gone for decades through these woods. Scampering over boulders and leaping far ahead, he would stay on the trail even far ahead of my sight. Soon though, he would be waylaid by a sniffing spot; he must stop. A minute or two later, I would plod along from behind, and then pass him, as he inhaled the local news. By the time I'd gone another 20 feet ahead, he would be right there at my side, then pass me again. We did this two-step dance for as long and as far as we could where there were no people on the quiet trails. Often, I outfitted him in his bright red Columbia dog jacket, partially for protection from the elements and briars, but mostly so as not to startle anyone we might come across in the woods. The jacket shouted out to any fellow hikers, *"I'm owned! I'm tame! Don't be afraid!"*

I could truly relax in the woods with him, because I knew there would not be any skateboards or other tiny wheels to trigger him into a frenzy. The candy red jacket also served to help him stand out against any hunters we might pass. A dead deer was about the only scent strong enough to entice him off the trail, and more than once he trotted back to me with a deer leg clamped in his jaws, the very image of a proud hunter.

Our very last long run was in 2016. Our life was on the cusp of major changes, though we didn't know it yet. Later that year Andrew and I bought our house together in Greenbelt, for which Baxter and I moved from Takoma Park to start our next adventure together. But on this chilly day in early March, we had work to do.

Baxter had been slowing down for a while now. At

nearly nine years old, he couldn't do the long miles we had done in the past, when we had run 13 miles together with gusto. On this day I had committed to cover eight miles of trail to flag a course for the next day's trail race, which was honestly pushing too far for him. I knew it may be too much but hadn't accepted it yet.

Getting to the trail was hard. There was heavy traffic, it was far away, and I was already tired before we had even started. I felt anxious about making a mistake and leading the runners astray on an important race, consulting the markings on my map multiple times and obsessing over correct placement of the flags before I had even left the car. I worried over how Baxter would sustain the trip and started out by leaving him in the car where he would just sleep while I was running (it was a cold winter day). But then I felt guilty for leaving him behind, so I resolved that he could do it slowly and turned back to the car to get him. As we crossed the busy road together from the parking lot, the trail opened through man-made sand dunes covered in tall grasses. This winding path protects the forest from the highway noise and the most immediate pollution. The turns of the dunes felt like walking a mandala, circling through a gateway before passing into the woods.

When we were finally settling into the woods, I began to relax a bit and enjoyed the solitude and the silence of the pines. Seemingly a world away, the stress and the traffic dropped far behind us. My anxiety melted off with every mile added. But I knew that we would not do this again – the distance required to reach these isolated parts of the forest was too much to ask of his aging legs. What would happen if he couldn't carry himself back out? Technically I could carry him, but his increasing age meant the risk had eclipsed the reward of these wild adventures.

The map marked the turning back point at a brook cutting through an open clearing. A freshly dead deer carcass was tangled up in the reeds. Five huge turkey vultures were busy at work on the carcass, pecking down onto it and then returning to a log on the ground that crossed the banks of the water. Baxter, off leash as always and well ahead of me, dove bark-first directly at the bald-headed turkey vultures. One single bird looked to be nearly his size, and with their wings fully spread on display in a horaltic pose, they were several times more impressive. I knew the birds were only interested in the dead meat, but their annoyance with this misguided canine might result in some projectile vomiting (their defense mechanism) causing an injury. I had no idea if they or he would attempt an attack. Baxter's only focus was on chasing off this unimaginable threat. I had to catch up on foot in order to get him away from them, because he was stubbornly ignoring my recall.

Birds from the sky that are as big as me? And they're eating a mammal on the ground?? My hackles shoot straight up as I let loose a ferocious flurry of non-stop barks. My ancient canine instincts take over as I crouch at the base of the log, frothy spittle flying, willing these birds to make the next move and end up crushed in my jaws.

The vultures, nonplussed, barely looked up from their meal. I collected my angry black dog from their wake, apologized for disturbing their lunch, and we turned back out of the wild woods.

JUST THE THREE OF US

BEFORE WE ALL LIVED TOGETHER, ANDREW LIVED IN A co-op townhouse in Greenbelt. We filled that house to the brim with music and friends, but with close neighbors and shared walls, we had to shut the music down before midnight. In order to flush the music-makers and merry-makers from the house, Andrew would propose we all go for a walk, ending with everyone taking their own way towards home. On this night we walked from his house down to a nearby playground. That night a spirit of whimsy took over, and we were soon swinging on the swings, tipping on the teeter-totter, and monkeying around on the bars.

Baxter circled around us all. I climbed up the slide tower of the tallest slide in the neighborhood, a drop of about 10 feet. Baxter followed me up the wide stair tower of the equipment. I thought it was cute. Then I planted my butt on the slide and slipped down. Baxter, lacking the anatomy to use a slide in the traditional way, followed me the only way that made sense to him, leaping after me without a moment's pause. No, he did not run down the slide, he leapt into the air as far as he could fly, straight out like Superman. He hit the slide at the bottom a split second after me. I didn't have eyes on him at the time, but Andrew saw him jump. He was there with me at the bottom, and in the middle was flying dog magic. I always knew he would follow me anywhere, and now I knew that included going straight off a cliff.

It was these kinds of unpredictable antics that always gave us something to talk about, a safe base to jump off from into a hard conversation. Throughout our years together, Baxter stood as a calming mediator for the relationship strife that had to be worked out between Andrew and me. His soft seal fur was always there to fall on when the answers that came back were too painful to hear. His fur absorbed more tears than every tissue I've ever used tallied up in total. We took many long walks with my heavy heart around our neighborhood at night. During every sad break-up (we had too many), Baxter was there, nestled on the couch in between us while we talked through what was lacking or what wasn't working in the relationship.

Then Baxter would do something silly and we'd share a laugh, melting a little bit of the ice that was swirling around the conversation. Those moments of levity allowed us to keep talking, listening, and working through it. It was hard. It took us years. We both had to grow to stand up inside our relationship, and we never would have been strong enough during those growing pains if Baxter hadn't given us his weight to rest on. His creatureliness delivered a closer connection to the world and to each other during those hard talks. I credit Baxter with helping us prepare the ground for our joyful wedding in 2018. Step by step and paw over paw, we did the work and found our way forward, together.

BAXTER'S SNOW DAY

My humans and I wake up together in the Green Place. My Lady opens the door to Outside and the world is cold, wet, and fluffy. I zoom around the Outside in a confused but joyful panic. Is this how the world is now? She lets me back into the Inside where we are warm and dry. Mr. A goes to the Outside and moves white piles around for a long time. When he comes back, I see there is a path leading from our den where I can see the brown Earth again, but everything around it is still covered in white.

Then both my humans put on a lot more clothing than usual. They look like marshmallow people. My Lady zips me into my snug red jacket. Paw, Paw, the flap wraps around the belly, zzzzzzzzzpptt, snap, snap, snap. I am locked into this fabric. I don't mind. The fuzzy fleece inside of it rubs softly against my belly and makes me feel warm. Clip – The Leash Is On! We go to the

Outside.

The white wet falling on my back doesn't feel cold when I wear the fabric. It's like it's not even touching me. My ear tips and paw paws are still chilly, but everything else is warm. Not too cold yet though, and we're on a mission. My humans grab some large pieces of plastic and drag these behind us over the white stuff. The stuff is deep, it comes up at least to my knees or deeper. We walk where the cars have cut tracks for us, still dragging the plastic behind. My sniffs are all crisp and sharp inside my snout. We pass a few other groups of humans with their tiny humans, but they are slow and tired, weighed down by their own marshmallow suits and walking in the other direction. I am not alarmed.

We are now standing at a precipice. My Lady releases the clip of the leash. I'm free to roam and sniff within her sight. Except then she makes the most foolish and dangerous miscalculation. Sitting on top of that sheet of plastic, she tips forward once, and is suddenly sucked over the edge! My Lady!! Without a thought for my own safety or self, I rush down the hill to save her. My humans are exceedingly foolish. Without me they would certainly die.

Barking directly behind her I run down the hill

at full speed, I must get in front of this plastic to stop it. She only picks up speed though, faster and faster, and I cannot grab hold of the edge to even slow her momentum. The slick ice crystals are pounded down under us like a speedway. I bark as she continues to slide further away from me, but I keep running so she is not abandoned in this terrifying moment. Why are humans so clumsy? How could this simple sheet of plastic even be able to steal one of them away? Finally, she slows, and comes to an ungraceful stop, plopping off the sheet and into the white stuff. I am there. I am licking to comfort her. I am there.

But only for one moment! Because in the next, Mr. A falls into the same trap!! Outrageous!!! I cannot be everywhere and save everyone all at once. I rush to his aid, barking at the cursed plastic. The humans are in a sort of daze, likely brought on by this white stuff, and have lost their kinesthetic sense of spatial reasoning.

The plastic sheets have bested them, and I fear for what will come next. Over and over, the humans clambered up the hill only to fall again at high speed. Each time I follow behind, barking, running, barking, begging the plastic to stop. Eventually, my paw paws are too frozen to carry me down one more time. I relent my chase. The humans are doomed. Still, I keep watch from the top of the hill as they continue to spin out. All that is left to me is prayer for their safe return to sanity. Eventually the cold sinks deeper into their delirium. They wake out of this manic state, collect the plastic sheets, pick up my lead, and my Lady, frozen, exhausted, but somehow contented, clips me back in and we return to the warm Den. Life resumes as if they had never been possessed by any spirits. This is the only time I will ever speak of obvious witchcraft in the Green Place.

EMERGENCIES

UP TO THIS POINT, YOU MAY HAVE HAD THE INCORRECT impression that Baxter was a healthy, if slightly gimpy, dog. As previously mentioned, the accident in his former life left him with two missing toes and metal rods holding his leg together underneath a scar that snaked up nearly the entire inside of his leg. Amazingly, these rods set well, and neither that nor the missing toes caused him any trouble.

But Baxter was not a healthy animal. Over the entirety of his life, this dog went on to spend tens of thousands of dollars at many different vets' offices under multiple near-death circumstances. The log of his health issues stretched across his entire life, starting from that first scare from the mystery scar and resulting bone infection. I have the credit card statements to show that I spent over $25,000 at veterinarians' offices, specialty surgeons, and urgent care clinics throughout his lifetime. Before I owned a dog, I would have said there was a limit to what I would be willing to spend at the vet's office. What I didn't expect was how the costs accrued over time, first a few hundred for one procedure, then another test for the doctors to learn more about the problem. Then maybe a week later, an emergency visit to the clinic – usually unrelated. It was never too much all at once, but it really added up. In the moment of crisis, you just want to pay whatever it costs and pray that the doctor's knowledge and abilities are sufficient to heal your friend. I'll never make the mistake of not carrying pet insurance again.

Oh no. No no no no no no no. What is wrong with me? This can't be happening. I can't believe this is happening. It's the middle of the night. My Lady is not waking up. Maybe if I stare at her a little while longer, she will feel my eyes on her and wake up. I would never bark to wake her, that would just be rude. I can't hold this in much longer. Nope, the staring is not working. She's still asleep. I'm just going to hop down the stairs quietly and see if I can sneak outside to the bathroom on my own, maybe one of the doors will be open somehow?

Oooohhh it's starting. I can't hold this together any longer. I am so embarrassed but what can I do? The front door – nope, it's locked. Let me check another door. No. Oh no oh no oh no I can't believe this is happening to me.

So it went all that night while we slept. When we woke up, the house was covered in a diarrhea trail leading out from our bedroom, down the stairs, and zig-zagging across the carpet, crossing from room to room, going from one door to another as Baxter had frantically tried to find a way outside during his silent crisis. He never made a sound to let me know. I later figured out that this time he had poisoned himself by licking too much of the flea and tick drops off of the fur of another dog. After that, we switched to edible preventives instead of the drops. But it wouldn't be long again before Baxter would find yet another creative way to land himself at the vet's office.

More than once there was a bill of several thousand dollars waiting for me at the check-out counter after a vet visit. He was wrapped in the cone so frequently that we decorated it with stickers and drawings, even adding an arrow pointing in the direction of his snout labeled "FOOD" (as in, food goes here!). More veterinarians than I could list have either saved his life or improved the quality of it. His treatment was world-class. He received TPLO knee surgery followed by months of physical therapy. He once had a colonoscopy and an endoscopy at the same time. I consulted a veterinarian who specialized in Chinese medicine for assistance with stabilizing his diet after he nearly died at six years old from lymphangiectasia. Add on the annual dental cleanings and routine mishaps and we were more than regular visitors to the vet clinic. Over the years he had lumps removed and tested for cancer, eventually became diabetic, had Cushing's Disease, and pancreatitis. Any one of those events could have killed him but veterinarians trained for many years to gain the specialty knowledge needed to save his life in all those instances. I am both grateful to have had the privilege of their knowledgeable care, and sad that this level of health care is something many humans around the world either cannot afford or will never have access to receive.

GREENBELT A.K.A.
THE GREEN PLACE

Before we can close the book of Baxter's life on this Earth, he has a few more years of adventures to recount. On Thanksgiving 2016, Andrew and I moved into a true dream house. We made the choice to move forward in life together, and Baxter and I became official Greenbelters. Andrew and I gained so much from this move, but Baxter arguably lost the most. At first, the house didn't have a fence, so overnight he lost the freedom to use the yard independently and could no longer bark along the sidewalk at passing pedestrians like he did from our Takoma Park house. This new house had a lot of stairs and slippery floors, and there was no play group for his afternoon adventures away from the house.

> When we lived in our tiny house, just the Lady and me, sometimes she had to leave me alone all day. I was more grown up by then, and mostly didn't destroy her things anymore, just a few cushions here and there when I had to take out

my rage about a passing skateboard. Most afternoons, a white van would pull up to our house and a nice lady named Krissy would come get me. I think my Lady knew Krissy, but I'm not sure how. In the back of Krissy's van were all of my afternoon friends. She drove us around the neighborhood, collecting dogs until there were 5 or 8 or 12 of us, and then she would take us to her house.

We squeezed in there like an old-timey dog catcher's cart, then played all afternoon. At the end of the day, we would pile back in the van and make the same route in reverse, dropping off each dog back to their house just in time for dinner. Sometimes it was dark when I got back home, and my Lady was already home waiting for me! JOY!! She said my social calendar was more booked than hers. Then the next day, back into the Magical Mystery Dog Van again.

Positive changes were happening too. I started working from home more regularly, and our new house was bursting with music and friends. Baxter enjoyed having frequent visitors. Every visitor received a fierce barking before coming in, and once inside he'd give a thorough sniff-down in the entryway, and only then were they admitted to the rest of the house.

Some nights he would follow me down the steep,

straight staircase to the basement music room and curl up at my feet under the drum kit. Even with the bass drum thumping against his ear drums, snare popping over his head, and cymbals crashing above him, he sat unphased. He was with me, doing his job. Other times he showed off his musical DJ scratching skills with his front paws digging rapidly for several minutes against the taut, smooth cushion of the futon. This goofy character we called DJ Baxxy-Bax. It only came out when he was feeling especially exuberant and serious at the same time. He was always a part of whatever was going on around the house, and in this way he cultivated his own wide circle of friends. I felt honored to be a witness to how far he'd come since those first days as a scared shelter pup. Baxter always carried himself with dignity and a whole-hearted dedication to his job, even when that job meant sitting under my feet, deafened under the drum set in the middle of a rock and roll song.

Our housewarming that next Spring had about 200 friends and neighbors passing through during the evening. Baxter made friends easily with visitors to the house, once they got inside the door. Direct friendships, independent from me. You did not become Baxter's friend because you and I were friends, but a person could earn Baxter's friendship. I was tangential and often not involved or even aware of all the relationships he held. He knew that visitors to our house were his guests, much like the foster dogs from years before. He charmed, indulged, and successfully begged for the tastiest morsels that he'd never get from me.

> Yes, we're at the fridge. Open it up. Right there in the drawer, you see the bag of deli turkey meat? The one Mr. A bought yesterday for his lunches this week? Hand it over to me quick. Sure, I'll do a little sit for that. Oh thank you. Yum yum yum.

> What do you mean you gave me ALL of it? Oh, Mr. A will not like that. I appreciate it, but we'll just keep this our little secret, OK?

One evening though, his begging caused a ruckus. In the new house, we continued the tradition of having an open door for musicians and friends, and friends of musicians on most Thursday nights. This allowed us to meet and play with lots of new people, and generally have a lot of fun. But this also meant that the first time we met many people was inside our house. Baxter always made it quite obvious that this was his house, and if you had a problem with that as part of the social gathering, you were welcome to not come in. Only one person out of the hundreds who have visited our house had that particular problem. I'm not sure if this person was afraid of dogs and didn't want to say it, or if she just wanted to stir up trouble. We met her at the door in the usual way and she somewhat hesitantly greeted the dog, and then proceeded to socialize with the other guests. I was busy in another conversation, so when she asked me if she could feed him a treat, I readily agreed but paid no close attention to this routine exchange of treats for petting.

As soon as I turned away from her, while we both were still in the kitchen, she shrieked out, "He bit me!"

Horrified, I turned back to them to face the gory truth. Had the monster inside his brain finally short-circuited? Would she need stitches? Had he snapped due to too many people around him? Would she sue us? All these thoughts appeared in my head during the millisecond it took to focus my attention back to the two of them. Baxter was still sitting there attentively, patiently expecting another treat. I looked down and examined the "bit" hand. It was perfectly intact, not a scratch. Still concerned, I pressed her for further details about this unprecedented event.

"Well, his tooth grazed my hand when I was giving him the treat."

Baxter's mouth had always been beyond gentle, so even this sounded surprising. Quickly I realized this was no more than a dramatic performance that I was not interested in attending. I removed Baxter from the room while I found Andrew to relate the events. Immediately, he knew what needed to be done and sprung to action.

He found her and stated plainly, "You need to leave."

She then attempted to argue and pulled back her initial reaction to explain that she was just startled, and that it was just the back of his tooth. But it didn't matter what else she said or tried to backpedal. Andrew was decided. He explained to her that it was nothing personal, but that she must leave because such an exclamation, beyond being untrue, was a real threat to our family. His resolute stance was rooted in the reasonable explanation that he did not dare risk finding out how little it might take to have our dog removed from us by the County Animal Control if she pursued this claim any further.

She left. The tension in the room deflated, and Baxter rejoined the gathering, nudging hands all around him for more petting and treats.

DINOSAUR PUPPY

THEN ALONG CAME IRIE. IRIE WILL HAVE HIS OWN ADVENtures to tell about in the future, so we will not dive into his tale here. For Baxter's story though, he represented literally the largest challenge of his life – rearing and taming a giant puppy, who grew to be four times the size of Baxter in a year or two. A real-life Clifford the Big Red Dog.

As we were settling into our beautiful new home, Andrew suffered two debilitating losses in short succession: his mother passed away unexpectedly, and we also lost a dear friend to cancer too young. We never got the opportunity to host a Thanksgiving or a birthday with his parents both together with us in the new house. A thick sadness settled in over us in mourning. It squeezed through the tiniest cracks, pressing down around us. Even while we felt so grateful to be in this place together, we were treading water in the pool filled up by Andrew's tears of loss. It is OK to mourn and to be sad, it is of course a necessary part of life. And life goes forward. A puppy was one thing I could do to bring some new life into our home, not to replace any sadness but to remind us that new things still grow and need our love. The sadness was so huge, a giant's heart was required.

A couple of months later circumstances aligned, and we brought home a 25 pound, 9-and-a-half-week-old ball of fluff and teeth – an Irish Wolfhound puppy. For the first few very short weeks (or was it days?), Irie could walk under Baxter. Both the puppy cuteness and the puppy teeth were nearly unbearable. Baxter tolerated him as he had all of his other dog guests, convinced at first that Irie was just a temporary visitor disrupting his peaceful retirement. Except this was a puppy unlike one any of us had ever encountered before, and he wasn't going anywhere.

WEEK 2

This puppy is so annoying, but he doesn't mean anything to me. Another house guest. Yes, yes, very cute. I can be gracious for a few days while he finds his new home in the world. I'll even share my treats and some great new toys too. Babies are fine for other people's houses, and I expect he will move out in a few days.

WEEK 3

Things really aren't adding up. For one, he's still

here and getting bigger every single day. His crate is strange. It's huge - you could fit two adult humans inside there. I've never seen anything like it. For another, my Lady and Mr. A spend entirely too much time and attention focused only on him.

She gets up at all hours of the night to take him outside. I stay in the bedroom, but this nonsense must stop. I'm losing sleep over it. I've started teaching him how to use the facilities like a proper dog, just until he leaves so things can go back to normal as soon as possible. I wonder how long this will go on until he leaves.

WEEK 5

The weirdest thing about him is how big he is getting, and so fast! Yesterday he was walking under me, but today I can walk under him! He really is the Most Obnoxious Creature I have ever met. I think my Lady has lost her mind bringing him here to bother us for so long.

MONTH 3

That's it. Weeks have now turned into months with this fuzzball. I really must start to lay down the law, as he is becoming more deeply embedded in my house every day that he stays here. I've patented a full training regimen to turn unruly, gigantic puppy-dogs into upstanding dog citizens and implementation starts TODAY. It will take every last bit of my patience, and more than a few carefully administered corrections, but I believe I am the only one in this household with the capacity to teach him all of the essentials of dog-human co-habitability and proper manners.

Whatever his breed, he will conform to my strict standards. As a graduate of my newly developed, patented program, he will become a Very Good Dog, no matter how much bigger he gets.

ONE YEAR LATER

He does have a few good qualities, even if he is completely spoiled rotten. He looks to me as his alpha guide through the world. I may, someday, begrudgingly call him a friend. As payment for services rendered, he drops $\frac{1}{4}$ to $\frac{1}{2}$ of all cookie crumbles for me out of his giant maw. I accept his tributes.

Mercifully, Irie did not pick up on Baxter's biggest fear of tiny wheels or general suspicion of the humans in the world outside our home. The few times on walks together when Irie saw Baxter deeply riled, Irie would play-attack Baxter, thinking it was a fun new game Baxter had initiated with him. Irie was unaware of the cause of the frenzy. As a puppy somewhere in the growth stages between 25 to 175 pounds, his play bows and vocalizations were a force that could not be ignored. This created an immediate distraction from the demon skateboard, conflicting and challenging Baxter's deepest held reactions. In those moments, he was forced to adapt. We even bought a skateboard around this time to desensitize the both of them to the sound. Irie was indifferent, and Baxter would look the other way when I was rolling around on it. This one reaction had become a tiny bit more selective over time.

Irie's size demanded a lot from all of us. Baxter managed as best he could. Time and puppy breath did their work in burning off the heaviest fog of sadness as life pulled all of us relentlessly forward.

2020.

THE SAME WEEKEND IN MARCH WHEN THE PANDEMIC panic shut down the whole East Coast of the United States, I had planned for a weekend trip to Ohio for a friend's wedding. Everything was retracting like a vacuum cord respooling. There were nearly universal flight and hotel cancelations, and schools and offices shuttered overnight. I made the decision to cancel my flight along with thousands of other intended travelers that weekend, as we began to navigate the many unknowns of the pandemic.

This ended up as a hidden blessing for us, because later that same weekend Baxter's health cratered. He was lethargic, had extreme diarrhea, and it seemed he could barely stand. I knew he was dehydrated or worse, so I rushed him to the emergency care clinic on a Sunday afternoon.

He was brought in by the vet tech while I sat in my car in the parking lot, nerves on edge, waiting for the office to call my number. We were not allowed to go inside the building. After the initial checks, his status was delivered to me outside in the parking lot, through our masks – masks that we felt lucky to have found lying around the house in those early pandemic days. The veterinarian rattled off a list of tests she needed to perform and fluids he needed pumped in. Hands shaky and reaching for the hand sanitizer after touching the pen and the clip board, I wasn't sure if I would collect my dog again when I left him there for overnight recovery. In a daze, I signed the intake forms and yet another $2,000 credit card receipt, then drove home without him.

Thanks to the miracle of modern veterinary medicine, he rallied. I got to bring him home. The vet diagnosed the cause of the acute pancreatitis crisis as both untreated diabetes and Cushing's Disease. All of this was news to me; I had no idea he had become diabetic. To make the situation worse, the drugs needed for this dual diagnosis were fighting against each other, making the correct insulin dosage a delicate and nearly impossible balance to manage. After I got past the shock of what a diagnosis of diabetes meant for our lives going forward, I accepted the vet tech's reassurance and learned how to administer the insulin shots he now required twice a day, every day. A strict feeding schedule was imposed because the shots had to be consistently 12 hours apart to be maximally effective. Treats were restricted in the extreme. His other daily drug and was so toxic to healthy people that the warning label said to not even touch it with bare hands if you were pregnant. All together I doled out to him what amounted to an elderly human's smorgasbord of daily medications.

These worthwhile efforts bought him six more good months. Still, I was seeing him slip away, losing strength every week, weighing less at each visit back to the vet. At first, I worried about how I would manage his additional care needs when work returned to our normal schedule of going back to the office. Slowly though, it became apparent to everyone that this was not a valid concern. As the pandemic continued to spread, offices across the world stayed closed. We stayed home. One real blessing from this time was that I spent every day working at my desk with Baxter curled up resting on my feet. His stoic heart beating there on my toes, safe.

Every day at lunch we walked together slowly, taking 30 minutes to leisurely amble to the edge of the street and back, a distance of five houses or so. It hardly seemed real that this was the same dog who would cover miles of trails with me in his younger years, but I had to accept the reality that sickness and age were now taking over as his gears downshifted.

All along the miles of walks and runs and sniffs, the new houses, the new puppy, the new husband, Baxter was my constant companion for all of it. He knew who he was and exactly where he fit in the world between his loves and fears, and his spot was always right at my feet. Now he was morphing into something different. Not demented or senile, but his edges had started to blur. He retained his beautiful seal coat and sharp bark, but shapeshifted into a softer, more pliable version of himself. In this way he drew my attention to the fact that he was growing old. At first so gradually, and then all in a rush.

Every day that it's sunny, we go to the park across the street, and I roll around on my back in the warm grass. I have a neat trick to keep my Lady from stopping me, I learned it a long time ago. Whenever I want to roll in something, I tuck my head into a forward tumble, like a gymnast on a mat routine. This way I can always get every sweet smell of mulch, grass, or some nice dead thing all over my back before my Lady can stop me.

Now I had no intention of stopping him, and happily, sometimes tearily, watched my old dog squeezing the best remaining parts of life out between the sunshine and the grass under his back. While he was rolling around, we were both there in that moment in the sun. The locked-down time at home ensured that I didn't miss a single day of this year away from my dogs, and I am so grateful for every single one of those days with him resting on my feet and our sunny lunch-time tumbles in the park.

FAREWELL TOUR

THE SAD CHAPTER OF BAXTER'S LAST WEEKEND ON EARTH is bizarre and fitting. Please feel free to skip this last section and leave him in your memory just where we were, rolling in the sunny, warm grass. It's hard to write and will be sad to read. But to see out his final hours together, we continue.

I made the decision that if I was going to see my family at all during the pandemic year, it would have to be before the holidays when the spread of COVID cases was predicted to be higher and families were discouraged from congregating across households. At the end of October 2020, Halloween weekend, I made a plan for visiting my sister that felt sufficiently distanced and safe. I packed up some festive Halloween garb to wear while tossing out candy to trick-or-treaters, copious layers against the cold, and Baxter's Bee costume. My sister gave him this yellow and black fuzzy costume with silver wings in his first year with me, and he wore it every Halloween of his life except this last one. I loaded up all this stuff into the car with Baxter to drive to New York, while Andrew and Irie stayed home.

Andrew offered and would have happily watched over Baxter for the few days I planned to be away, but he still seemed strong enough to travel, and my entire family looked forward to seeing him again, even though we knew it may be for the last time. We had just been in to see the vet that week for his routine shots and check-up, were he received an encouraging report of stable health. I felt reassured that he could do this last trip, although I was fully aware of his deteriorating health. This was an opportunity for my New York family to say goodbye to the dog they also knew well and loved.

The social distancing plan we had decided upon was for Baxter and me to stay alone in my sister's vacant house. My sister and her husband own two houses in the same village, located adjacent to one another. The second house was purchased and they moved into it so that extensive renovations could begin on their historic stone house, built in 1816. After their move, the stone house was still frequently used during this year as a guest house for visitors. In normal times I would never have stayed there alone during my visit, I would have stayed at my parents' home, but given that I had this ideal option to remain distanced from other households it made sense to use it. I've always known this place as my sister's home. When I imagine what she is doing at any random moment, I imagine her here. They've lived there for over two decades of marriage, and so it felt incredibly strange that their master bedroom turned guest room is where I was set up to stay. While the plan made perfect sense on paper during a pandemic, it also read like the intro to a low-budget horror movie: Woman travels from out of town, checks into a historic, probably haunted house on Halloween weekend to stay alone, isolated away from others, with only her elderly dog for companionship. What could possibly go wrong?

None of us imagined Baxter would not be coming home with me. He and I had made this trip together so many times. He did not eat the morning of our departure, but this wasn't too far out of the ordinary, as he often skipped one of his two meals during the days when he was feeling worse. Then he was completely lackluster on the drive up, staying so very still that I was concerned he had stopped breathing once or twice as I glanced back at him through the rear-view mirror. After we arrived, he didn't eat dinner either and I grew more concerned, but I hoped he would eat the next day after he had settled in. The vet had advised me not to offer any food other than his prescription diet unless he didn't eat for more than two days, and then to call them. He had never gone that long though without eating. When he didn't eat again on Saturday morning, even with a variety of delicious-smelling cat foods offered to entice his appetite, I knew things had become grave.

Unless he ate, I could not administer his insulin.

More than just not eating, he was barely moving. The Friday night that we arrived at my parents' house and stretched our legs after the 8-hour drive, there was no burst of energy, not even a glimmer of excitement. I like to think there was a whiff of recognition embedded in the scents of their house, and that the familiar voices of family surrounded him with memories of healthier days. But he was too sick and too tired. He was ready to leave us.

On the Saturday of my visit I drove back to my parents' home so Baxter could spend the day with them while I was busy with my sister. On the way I saw my childhood best friend and her family standing outside chatting in her parents' driveway, so I pulled over for a quick hello. They knew him well from his younger years and many summers in New York. Serendipitously, this trip had expanded into a kind of farewell parade, making brief stops to see so many who loved him before moving on. I opened the car door, they looked into his clouded eyes, and everyone knew it was time to say goodbye.

THE GIFTS

IF I HAD BEEN AT HOME IN GREENBELT ON THIS DAY, I likely would have made a different decision on this Halloween morning. It's impossible to speculate on the other outcomes. But Brenda and I had made a commitment to volunteer at an outdoor event, this was the only day since January I had seen my sister, and it was the only full day I would see her all year due to the pandemic. So we stuck with the original plan and carried out our activities while he rested with my parents, which seemed like a reasonable option at the time. But by the time trick-or-treating had ended and I returned to collect him that evening, it was clear that he may not last through the night.

Despite all of his illnesses and failing health over these last six months especially, I wasn't prepared for this. The vet earlier in the week had not warned me about this, and I had no idea what the end would look like. I had no plan. I didn't give enough thought to how things would end. I wish I would have given him that. He didn't just go to sleep and not wake up. I didn't think about how hard it would be for him to die.

Back in the vacant house, Brenda sat with Baxter and I in her bedroom that I was borrowing. Distanced but together, we cried. Eventually she retired to bed, and I tried to sleep but continued to cry. He continued to hold on. I had blankets and towels laid out all over the slippery floor, but these were useless. I tried to keep him still by holding him, but each time I was away for a moment he would try to stand. The wood floor was like ice under his wobbly legs and he would collapse again. During the middle of the night he lost control of his bodily functions. The tiny hope that had lingered in my mind that this could be reversed once we could get to a vet dissipated in the moment when the fluids leaked out of him in a hot stream over my arms, seeping into the cracks of the antique, polished wooden floor. I swaddled his lower half in the towels and blankets I could find and just held him so he wouldn't try to get up again. In the early morning hours Brenda brought more towels while she ran the soiled blankets through the laundromat so we would not run out. My sister gave Baxter and I the first gift that night, the gift of emotional comfort and caring for his last physical needs.

On this, his last night on Earth, Baxter and I were together as we'd been on our very first night. Isolated away from the larger, fuller life we had built in Maryland, we were transported back in time to the intimate space where it was just the two of us once again, as we'd started out. But now it was to face the ultimate task of dying. His physical letting go. I had never seen or experienced this before; it felt otherworldly. But even here he was teaching me the very essence of life while I witnessed his transition. Always stubborn, he clung on all night and into the next morning, Sunday. The events of that night had frozen me. I felt catatonic, incapable of making the necessary decision. Speaking with Andrew over the phone, he told me very firmly that I could not allow another night to pass this way. These words motivated me out of my sadness and into action. Andrew gave me the gift of clarity to act.

Every local veterinary office was closed on Sunday. After some frantic texting with friends to find anyone to help, I called their livestock vet at home in the early morning hours, but he didn't pick up the phone. The only veterinary option was an hour's drive away, and with no exaggeration, a snowstorm was on the horizon. In order to return safely home to Maryland, I needed to beat this storm or risk driving in hazardous conditions through the mountains of Pennsylvania. A decision was made, and my family helped me carry it out. Finally, we had a plan.

I had six hours left to pack up, handle the vet visit, then push it out of my mind while I completed the drive ahead of the storm. Leaving at that very moment left little time to spare. Implementing the plan, my parents followed behind my car to the vet's office in their car.

After the euthanasia was completed, they collected Baxter and laid his still-warm body in the trunk of their car, then drove him back to their house to bury. He was buried under the blueberry bushes where he loved to nibble and steal the berries, and next to our other beloved former family pets. My parents gave him the gift of a peaceful, permanent resting place.

We made the trip to the vet as described. After the vet administered an initial sedative of light anesthesia, she left Brenda and I in the room together with him to say the final goodbye before she would return to administer the lethal dose. Instead of accepting this, in the few moments while the vet had stepped away, Baxter fully and finally relaxed. His body took one last full shudder and sigh. This was his gift to me: leaving on his own terms. As life left him, he shape-shifted for the final time to receive his wings, because all dogs go to heaven – Right?

OVER THE BRIDGE

I flew up here fast. This is great. My fur is baked hot to the touch in these sunny spots through the clouds. The grass smells so sweet and there are dead things and mulch to roll in everywhere.

Hey! You other dogs!! Settle Down. Stop fooling around! No roughhousing. I won't tolerate your silly games in my heaven! Get in line and act right. I always did love to boss around the other dogs on Earth when we played. Now I get to do it all the time! Oh, what's that scent? Just-born baby bunnies? Let me have a quick sniff and a squeak. Adult bunnies too?? Get out of here!! I'll catch them soon too.

Wait. What's this sidewalk doing here. Oh no. Oh no. Oh no. Tiny wheels cranking across cement. Not In My Heaven! I'll get that skateboard once and for all. A whole skatepark full of them too. They can't escape any more. I will finally have my

Revenge!! When I catch one though, I'm not sure what I'll do then...

AWARDS CEREMONY

Baxter always had a primal heart underneath his domestication. He was built to survive. Like "Dog", Mad Max's companion, he was constantly on guard and ready to spring to action. His instinct was to protect the pack, and to protect me. In reality, the biggest threats he ever had to face were the fears inside his mind, and he took these anxieties out on his biggest prey – two couches and the backseat of a Toyota Corolla.

But much like any refined country gentleman, Baxter practiced hunting and foraging as evidence that he retained his ancient skills, encoded genetically over centuries. I don't glorify his hunting in these pages; I never approved of it. But in all fairness to showcase his notable lifetime achievements and award the proper accolades, I've allowed him to recount his most memorable animal trophies for you here:

- 🐾 *Excellence in Mousing* – I caught many a trespassing mouse. I must have some Jack Russell Terrier in my blood. If I couldn't reach the critter, I would plant my body directly in the midst of the strongest scent and snort deep, terrifying snuffles. To the mouse's ears, the wolf was at the door.

🐾 *Swiftest Squirrel Swallower* – I once gulped down an entire dead squirrel. It had been killed during the night, maybe dropped there by an owl. The blood spots were fresh in the snow that morning. I didn't think about it at all. I slurped it down whole the minute I found it.

🐾 *Prized Deer Parts Collector* – I would often find a stray deer leg during our trail runs to gnaw on. Once, in New York, I wandered off into the woods alone and returned dragging a full "five-point rack" shed by a buck. Cautiously, Grandpa hung it in a tree for a few weeks in front of the house as an offering to any disgruntled hunters searching for this possibly stolen prize. When no humans stepped forward to make a claim, Grandpa took a hacksaw to it and cut it up for me into chew toys. My Lady says a single small piece of this antler can cost $10 or $20 at the pet store, so she was pleased with only this one prize.

🐾 *Blue Ribbon Baby Bunny Butcher* – I once killed an entire warren of just-born baby bunnies. They dared to build their nest right outside the front door of our Den! As I squeaked the life out of all of them one by one, each exhaled a single tiny puff of last breath that sounded exactly like my favorite squeaker toys. The dumb bunnies never even tried to run away; in less than a minute it was over.

🐾 ***Third Place Turtle Menacer –*** I stayed sharp through my last summer of life. While my Mr. A and my Lady were relaxing on the deck, I hopped down the stairs, drawn to a small, dragging commotion through the pile of leaves in the yard. After about 30 minutes Mr. A grew suspicious and found me in the far corner of the yard gnawing on the corner of a medium-sized yellow and brown box turtle's shell. I had grasped the very much alive turtle and flipped it upside down. Holding it between my paws, I was masticating a corner of the shell with my powerful back jaws to get at the tucked-in legs and head. If not for Mr. A's meddling, I would have had the shell softened up enough to grab ahold of some fresh turtle meat that day.

To balance out this list of "achievements", I feel I must note what Baxter omitted. His biggest embarrassment resulting from his encounters with wildlife, which happened only once.

He was skunked.

BEAR HUGS

As I was wrapping up writing this, I was surprised to find that he also looks back in on our side of the Rainbow Bridge every once in a while, though I really shouldn't be surprised. Baxter has visited my dreams a few times since he passed, as an image, a friendly glimpse, or a jingle of his collar. In this latest dream he appeared to communicate directly to me from the other side.

In the dream, Andrew and I are laying around the living room watching television with Irie nearby. It's a completely realistic dream setting where everything is happening exactly as it does in real life, and you can't distinguish that you are even in a dream. We hear a noise coming from the back hallway where the dogs are let in and out from the backyard. The noise is a common dog sound, nails clicking on the laminate flooring.

I look down the hallway and I see Baxter approaching us. I rise to my knees but don't get up, waiting in shock as he approaches me. I start squeaking a series of high-pitched "Hi Hi Hi Hi Hi's" to draw his attention to me, but he doesn't need the extra encouragement. As he comes closer his head is lolling, bobbing like a happy cow. He moves easily, with no pain. He meets me where I'm kneeling on the orange carpet of our living room and presses his full body weight against my chest, head-first and tucked down. He did this many times in life when he was especially happy to see me, usually after a long separation. I've read this is the dog's behavioral equivalent to wrapping their arms around you in a warm bear hug. The joy in that second overpowers my body and shatters the dream state. I awake with one more "Hi" whispered out loud and tears of gratitude to have hugged him once more.

I won't know when he'll appear again, but I know he will. I'll always carry him in my heart. A dog so fully committed to the serious business of living can't stay away for long.

ACKNOWLEDGEMENTS

THIS BOOK WOULD NOT EXIST WITHOUT THE FOLLOWING people to thank. The Internet can be a great connector, so I have never met in person the people who worked on this book. I reached out to these talented professionals with my idea for this project on the way to becoming a real book, and they all saw something in the idea that sparked a connection and a willingness to help bring it into the world. Jill Southworth designed the cover illustration. Thank you for your awesome auction item donation to Wolfhound World, and for then taking my real photograph of Baxter and infusing it with magic and mystery. Sarah Lamb and Sydney Wilson, thank you for your copy editing and your detailed notes on flow. Your ideas for reorganizing certain sections really improved the readability of this story, and your feedback gave me reassurance that it was interesting to people outside my inner circle when I was feeling it might not be worthwhile to share. That input was so motivating to me to keep working. Thank you to Susan Veach for professional page layout and cover design. The minute I connected with you I knew this was really going to be something I could add to my bookshelf someday!

On the personal side, thank you to my Dad for the title of the book, and especially for sharing your love of personal storytelling throughout my entire life. Thank you to Heather for sharing your clever phrasing and insight about dogs over the years, and of course for our running dog-themed text string of things our dogs are doing at any moment. Thanks to Rob for sparking the idea that anyone can publish a book; I didn't need any special approvals to do it. Thanks to my Mom and Dad, Brenda and Stu, Brent and Stacey and the girls for always asking me about how Baxter's life was going whenever we talked and being genuinely interested in what he was up to that week. And of course, thanks enduringly to my husband Andrew who fully encouraged this effort, advised me on next steps, and put up with all my lost sleep while writing it.

CPSIA information can be obtained
at www.ICGtesting.com
Printed in the USA
BVHW041255211021
619553BV00012B/344

9 781737 426905